The Learning Works

Analogy Challenge

Test-Prep Exercises • 3 Levels of Difficulty • Grades 5-8

Written by Linda Schwartz • Illustrated by Bev Armstrong

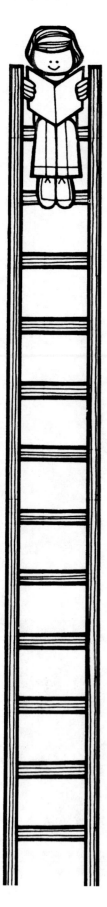

The Learning Works

Typesetting and Editorial Production:
Clark Editorial & Design

Copyright © 2000

Creative Teaching Press, Inc.
Huntington Beach, CA 92649

ISBN: 0-88160-354-6

LW 393

Printed in the United States of America.

Introduction

Analogy Challenge helps students to analyze, solve, and write analogies. The exercises in this book provide practice in analyzing relationships between words and strengthening students' vocabularies, both skills critical for standardized testing.

The exercises include analogies based on the following concepts:

- parts of speech (nouns, verbs, adjectives, adverbs)
- synonyms
- antonyms
- homophones
- recognized parts of a whole
- male and female counterparts
- tools and the occupations with which they are associated
- and special topics such as food, animals, people, and sports

For your convenience, the book is divided into three levels of difficulty ranging from easier to more difficult. This format will help you tailor the exercises to best meet the ability levels and needs of your students.

As an added bonus, the book contains an Answer Sheet (page 52) that can be reproduced and used with each exercise. This enables students to practice filling in their answers using the "bubble" format found on most standardized tests. Also included are pages where students can create their own analogies using dictionaries, thesauruses, and other reference materials. An answer key is provided at the back of the book.

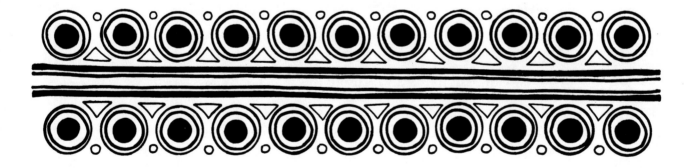

Contents

Contents

(continued)

Level 3 - Analogies ◆ 39–51

About Analogies

What Is an Analogy?
An **analogy** is a relationship between one pair of words or terms that serves as the basis for the creation of another pair of words or terms. If the analogy has been completed correctly, the terms in the second pair have the same relationship to each other as do the terms in the first pair.

What Are These Relationships?
The relationships that form the basis for the completion of analogies vary from one analogy to another. The pairs may be **synonyms**—words that have the same meaning, **antonyms**—words that have opposite meanings, or **homophones**—words that have the same sound but have different spellings and meanings. One term in the pair may name the **group** of which the other term is a **member**. Or one term may name a **whole** of which the other term is a recognized **part**.

In order for the analogy to be correct, the relationship between the terms in the first pair of words must be exactly the same as the words in the second pair. For example, if the terms in the first pair are synonyms and the terms in the second pair are antonyms, no analogy exists among the four terms.

How Do You Write an Analogy?
Analogies are usually written in the following form:

generous is to *selfish* as *fragile* is to *sturdy*

To shorten this form, a single colon (:) is sometimes used in place of the words *is to*, and a double colon (: :) is used in place of the word a*s*, to separate the two pairs that make up the analogy.

generous : selfish : : fragile : sturdy

About Analogies
(continued)

How Do You Complete an Analogy?
Read the first pair of terms and think about the relationship between them. Are the terms synonyms or antonyms? Are they homophones? Is one a recognized part of the other or a member of the group named by the other?

Example:
divulge : disclose : : tranquil : _____

    a. noisy
    b. boisterous
    c. trustworthy
    d. peaceful

In this example, the words *divulge* and *disclose* are synonyms—they mean the same thing. The synonym for the word *tranquil* is **d. peaceful**.

Example:
brood : birds : : herd : _____

    a. hawks
    b. elephants
    c. dogs
    d. whales

In this example, *brood* names the group that *birds* belong to. The correct answer is **b. elephants**, because elephants belong to a group called a *herd*.

Example:
nose : head : : nail : _____

    a. finger
    b. hammer
    c. eyes
    d. hair

In this example, a *nose* is found on a *head*. The correct answer is **a. finger** because a nail is found on a finger.

Example:
llama : mammal : : pheasant : _____

    a. pleasant
    b. pigeon
    c. bird
    d. fish

In this example, a *llama* is a kind of *mammal*. Thus, mammal names the group of which llama is a member. What word names the *group* of which *pheasant* is a member? The correct answer is **c. bird**.

Example:
pin : cushion : : letter : _____

    a. box
    b. envelope
    c. mail
    d. sew

In this example, a *cushion* holds a pin. What holds a letter? The correct answer is **b. envelope.**

Analogy Practice

Here's a chance for you to practice doing analogies. Follow these easy steps.

1. Decide if the relationship between the words in the first pair is **synonyms**, **antonyms**, or **homophones**.

2. Write one of these three words on the line below the analogy as shown.

3. Look at the first word in the second pair and decide which one of the lettered answer choices is related to it in the same way. Underline this answer choice as shown.

> *Example:*
> permanent : temporary : : guilty : _____
>
> _____**antonyms**_____
>
>   a. accountable
>   b. responsible
>   c. <u>innocent</u>
>   d. blame

1. bashful : shy : : tardy : _____

   _____

       a. prompt
       b. late
       c. early
       d. cautious

2. flower : flour : : ewe : _____

   _____

       a. animal
       b. mammal
       c. you
       d. few

3. ignite : extinguish : : flexible : _____

   _____

       a. floppy
       b. feeble
       c. circular
       d. rigid

4. bargain : negotiate : : previous : _____

   _____

       a. after
       b. specific
       c. prior
       d. private

Analogy Practice

(continued)

The following analogies will give you practice in doing other types of analogies you'll find in the book. Some are words that name male and female counterparts such as *gander : goose : : rooster : hen.* Some show the relationship of offspring to a particular animal such as *cub : bear : : kitten : cat.* Other analogies are names given to an animal group such as *swarm : bees : : covey : quail.* You'll get practice in analogies dealing with parts to a whole, individual members of a larger group, tools and the occupations with which they are customarily associated, shades of colors, and more. In each practice exercise below, underline the word that best completes the analogy.

1. rhodamine : red : : ebony :
   a. blue
   b. green
   c. white
   d. black

2. rafter : turkeys : : gaggle :
   a. geese
   b. wolves
   c. monkeys
   d. choke

3. telescope : astronomer : : microscope :
   a. laboratory
   b. scientist
   c. observatory
   d. planets

4. stallion : mare : : bull :
   a. cattle
   b. steer
   c. horse
   d. cow

Sometimes analogies are written in the following format:

colt : horse : :
a. chicken : turkey
b. bird : pigeon
c. gosling : goose
d. pelican : beak

The correct answer is **c. gosling : goose** because the relationship in both pairs of words is the offspring of the animal named.

Complete the practice exercises below. Underline the word that best completes each analogy.

5. nape : neck : :
   a. arm : shoulder
   b. heel : heal
   c. elbow : finger
   d. heel : foot

6. emerald : green : :
   a. yellow : color
   b. beige : brown
   c. amber : green
   d. peach : fruit

7. enamel : tooth : :
   a. root : leaf
   b. nose : ear
   c. pupil : eye
   d. scalp : brush

Analogy Challenge
© The Learning Works, Inc.

Analogy Practice

(continued)

What happens when you don't know the meaning of the words used in an analogy? How can you figure out the analogy? If you cannot identify the relationship between the words or terms in a pair, look them up in a dictionary. You may learn about a definition of which you have been unaware and, in doing so, discover how the words are related.

In the analogies below, you will probably find several words that are unfamiliar to you. Look up these words. Identify the relationship between the words in the first pair. On the line provided, write the word that names this relationship. Underline the word that best completes each analogy.

1. panacea : remedy : : querulous : _____

   _____ synonyms _____

   a. quarry
   b. ominous
   c. fretful
   d. placid

2. loquacious : taciturn : : cooperative : _____

   _____ antonyms _____

   a. repetitious
   b. tedious
   c. reclusive
   d. recalcitrant

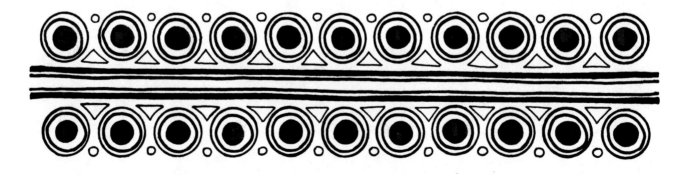

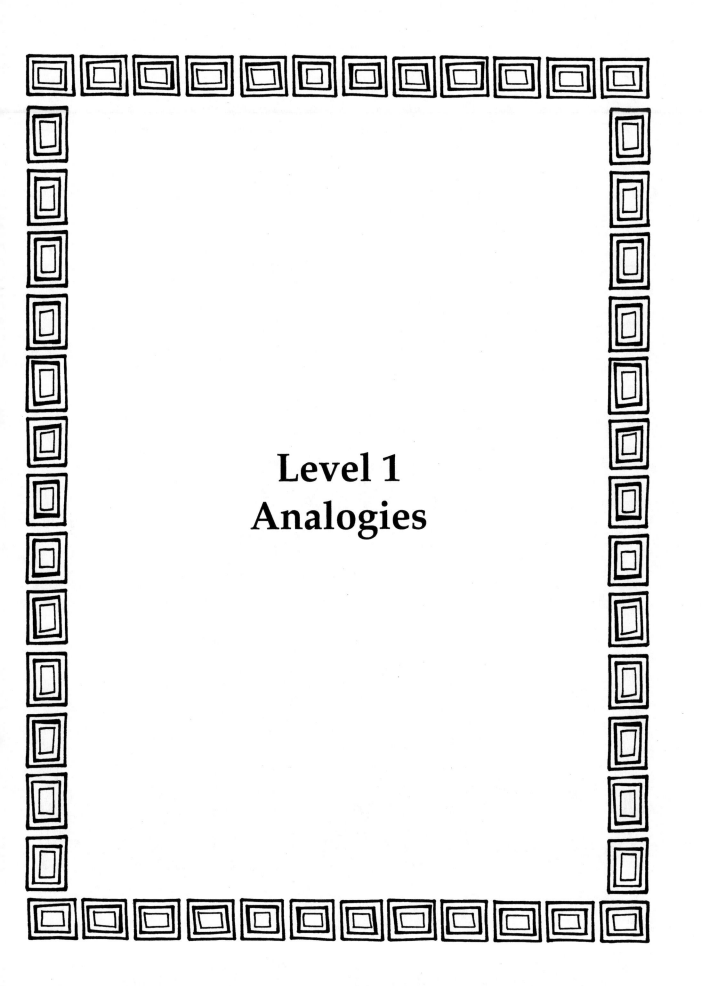

Level 1
Analogies

Nouns

Instructions: Underline the word that best completes each analogy.
On the Answer Sheet, fill in the bubbles that match your answers.

1. finger : hand : : toe :
   a. leg
   b. nail
   c. bone
   d. foot

2. parchment : paper : : robin :
   a. bird
   b. red
   c. reptile
   d. wren

3. bow : arrow : : bat :
   a. base
   b. hat
   c. mammal
   d. ball

4. taxi : cab : : automobile :
   a. train
   b. truck
   c. car
   d. motorcycle

5. tape : listen : : newspaper :
   a. read
   b. magazine
   c. book
   d. music

6. cargo : freight : : route :
   a. road
   b. street
   c. course
   d. globe

7. load : lode : : vein :
   a. blood
   b. artery
   c. leaf
   d. vane

8. hat : head : : sandals :
   a. shoes
   b. feet
   c. beach
   d. socks

9. dictionary : words : : atlas :
   a. world
   b. postcards
   c. encyclopedia
   d. maps

10. polka : dance : : ukulele :
    a. song
    b. hula
    c. instrument
    d. guitar

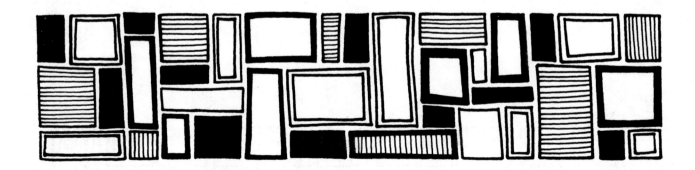

Name_____

Verbs

Instructions: Underline the word that best completes each analogy.
On the Answer Sheet, fill in the bubbles that match your answers.

1. assist : aid : : purchase :
   a. push
   b. return
   c. buy
   d. sell

2. close : open : : include :
   a. omit
   b. add
   c. comprise
   d. involve

3. start : stop : : decrease :
   a. diminish
   b. reduce
   c. increase
   d. decry

4. mend : repair : : swerve :
   a. serve
   b. offer
   c. twist
   d. laugh

5. elect : choose : : imitate :
   a. inquire
   b. identify
   c. include
   d. copy

6. build : billed : : chews :
   a. eats
   b. chose
   c. choose
   d. bites

7. inquire : ask : : modify :
   a. moderate
   b. moisten
   c. alter
   d. muddle

8. quiver : shake : : vanish :
   a. enter
   b. disappear
   c. transform
   d. emerge

9. forget : remember : : shrink :
   a. shrivel
   b. shock
   c. rink
   d. swell

10. pound : beat : : sulk :
    a. slink
    b. pay
    c. pout
    d. browse

Analogy Challenge
© The Learning Works, Inc.

Name_____

Adjectives

Instructions: Underline the word that best completes each analogy.
On the Answer Sheet, fill in the bubbles that match your answers.

1. absent : present : : young :
   a. childish
   b. old
   c. new
   d. youthful

2. petite : tiny : : enormous :
   a. huge
   b. many
   c. microscopic
   d. entire

3. rich : poor : : fragile :
   a. speedy
   b. flimsy
   c. sturdy
   d. delicate

4. mean : kind : : fresh :
   a. smart
   b. original
   c. homemade
   d. stale

5. happy : sad : : ambitious :
   a. eager
   b. lazy
   c. crooked
   d. absurd

6. previous : former : : messy :
   a. modern
   b. clean
   c. massive
   d. sloppy

7. severe : harsh : : rapid :
   a. sluggish
   b. watery
   c. fast
   d. repetitious

8. casual : formal : : difficult :
   a. easy
   b. hard
   c. delightful
   d. doubtful

9. dry : parched : : genuine :
   a. groundless
   b. real
   c. vacant
   d. brave

10. sensible : wise : : tranquil :
    a. touchy
    b. noisy
    c. peaceful
    d. evil

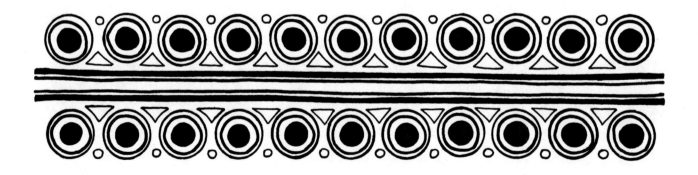

Name_____

Adverbs

Instructions: Underline the word that best completes each analogy.
On the Answer Sheet, fill in the bubbles that match your answers.

1. on : off : : always :
   a. already
   b. never
   c. about
   d. now

2. often : seldom : : weakly :
   a. weekly
   b. usually
   c. strongly
   d. feebly

3. beneath : above : : before :
   a. previously
   b. after
   c. barely
   d. hastily

4. inwardly : outwardly : : daintily :
   a. rapidly
   b. moderately
   c. petitely
   d. clumsily

5. timidly : shyly : : happily :
   a. sadly
   b. mournfully
   c. joyfully
   d. hopefully

6. jointly : separately : : kindly :
   a. cruelly
   b. friendly
   c. closely
   d. cautiously

7. easily : simply : : wisely :
   a. foolishly
   b. sensibly
   c. safely
   d. timely

8. noisily : quietly : : quickly :
   a. quaintly
   b. speedily
   c. slowly
   d. rapidly

9. yearly : annually : : honestly :
   a. hopelessly
   b. truthfully
   c. falsely
   d. keenly

10. commonly : rarely : : loosely :
    a. wobbly
    b. sparsely
    c. lightly
    d. tightly

Review of Parts of Speech

Instructions: Underline the word that best completes each analogy.
On the Answer Sheet, fill in the bubbles that match your answers.

1. gloomily : cheerfully : : quietly :
   a. peacefully
   b. neglectfully
   c. visibly
   d. noisily

2. swipe : steal : : guard :
   a. protect
   b. give
   c. grade
   d. upset

3. water : liquid : : air :
   a. cloud
   b. sky
   c. gas
   d. solid

4. candy : sweet : : lemon :
   a. fruit
   b. sour
   c. yellow
   d. lime

5. risk : danger : : occur :
   a. depart
   b. present
   c. happen
   d. approach

6. peak : peek : : veil :
   a. valley
   b. lace
   c. bride
   d. vale

7. caution : warn : : launch :
   a. lunge
   b. drive
   c. break
   d. start

8. sing : choir : : march :
   a. month
   b. parade
   c. drum
   d. travel

9. week : year : : quart :
   a. gallon
   b. pint
   c. pound
   d. inch

10. real : genuine : : counterfeit :
    a. number
    b. money
    c. fake
    d. worth

Synonyms

Instructions: Underline the word that best completes each analogy.
On the Answer Sheet, fill in the bubbles that match your answers.

1. begin : start : :
   a. control : contempt
   b. calm : noisy
   c. caution : warn
   d. clear : hazy

2. huge : vast : :
   a. keen : sharp
   b. dull : knife
   c. start : end
   d. blade : grass

3. search : seek : :
   a. thin : fat
   b. damp : dry
   c. dense : thick
   d. frightening : fretting

4. idle : lazy : :
   a. tight : slack
   b. support : supply
   c. praise : criticism
   d. taunt : ridicule

5. singe : burn : :
   a. loose : rigid
   b. precise : exact
   c. premature : late
   d. preoccupied : attentive

6. clumsy : awkward : :
   a. congenial : comical
   b. emphatic : envious
   c. atrocious : outrageous
   d. attractive : ugly

7. mentor : coach : :
   a. rivalry : competition
   b. bravery : cowardice
   c. defense : offense
   d. rejection : acceptance

8. fool : trick : :
   a. fixate : please
   b. deceive : decry
   c. pardon : forgive
   d. loathing : loving

9. purchase : buy : :
   a. depressed : agitated
   b. punctual : prompt
   c. brave : hero
   d. important : insignificant

10. odd : peculiar : :
    a. whimsical : serious
    b. compatible : collected
    c. obedient : sad
    d. radiant : brilliant

Antonyms

Instructions: Underline the word that best completes each analogy.
On the Answer Sheet, fill in the bubbles that match your answers.

1. join : separate : : vanish :
   a. forbid
   b. leave
   c. appear
   d. close

2. early : late : : foe :
   a. failure
   b. friend
   c. enemy
   d. fear

3. allow : forbid : : vague :
   a. vogue
   b. exact
   c. violent
   d. hasty

4. victory : defeat : : temporary :
   a. tame
   b. zealous
   c. moderate
   d. permanent

5. tiny : colossal : : meager :
   a. skimpy
   b. melodious
   c. ample
   d. join

6. fresh : stale : : seldom :
   a. rarely
   b. nowhere
   c. hasty
   d. often

7. plentiful : scarce : : flimsy :
   a. solid
   b. opaque
   c. polite
   d. beneficial

8. advance : retreat : : exterior :
   a. empty
   b. irregular
   c. interior
   d. exit

9. minimum : maximum : : lenient :
   a. inferior
   b. harsh
   c. shallow
   d. illegal

10. soft : loud : : polite :
    a. kind
    b. proven
    c. pleasant
    d. rude

Name_____

Review of Synonyms and Antonyms

Instructions: Underline the word that best completes each analogy.
On the Answer Sheet, fill in the bubbles that match your answers.

1. positive : negative : : offense :
   a. officer
   b. defense
   c. defeat
   d. doubt

2. obsolete : current : : rigid :
   a. stiff
   b. tense
   c. flexible
   d. difficult

3. teach : instruct : : jump :
   a. leap
   b. include
   c. imagine
   d. clear

4. reject : accept : : complex :
   a. complete
   b. simple
   c. apart
   d. difficult

5. sparkle : gleam : : fortify :
   a. forget
   b. weaken
   c. recall
   d. strengthen

6. normal : ordinary : : blank :
   a. brave
   b. empty
   c. full
   d. worth

7. fresh : stale : : heavy :
   a. bulky
   b. ample
   c. careless
   d. light

8. legitimate : legal : : valiant :
   a. vagrant
   b. timid
   c. brave
   d. vacant

9. active : passive : : join :
   a. link
   b. separate
   c. arrive
   d. benefit

10. resist : comply : : cheerful :
    a. happy
    b. calm
    c. somber
    d. gleeful

Name_____

Food

Instructions: Underline the word that best completes each analogy.
On the Answer Sheet, fill in the bubbles that match your answers.

1. apple : fruit : : asparagus :
   a. green
   b. fruit
   c. vegetable
   d. stalk

2. toast : bread : : barbecue :
   a. fire
   b. grill
   c. marinade
   d. hamburger

3. freeze : defrost : : simmer :
   a. boil
   b. glaze
   c. fillet
   d. smoke

4. spaghetti : meatballs : : jelly :
   a. jam
   b. peas
   c. peanut butter
   d. candy

5. coffee : beverage : : paprika :
   a. spice
   b. cinnamon
   c. vegetable
   d. fruit

6. carrot : vegetable : : cantaloupe :
   a. round
   b. fruit
   c. meat
   d. poultry

7. mix : blend : : odor :
   a. order
   b. chef
   c. smell
   d. burn

8. shell : egg : : peel :
   a. hamburger
   b. banana
   c. ice cream
   d. bread

9. tasteless : flavorful : : tender :
   a. meat
   b. render
   c. soft
   d. tough

10. stove : kitchen : : bed :
    a. sleep
    b. bedroom
    c. night
    d. blanket

Name_____

Animals

Instructions: Underline the word that best completes each analogy.
On the Answer Sheet, fill in the bubbles that match your answers.

1. feather : bird : :
   a. insect : ant
   b. scale : fish
   c. duck : quack
   d. dog : puppy

2. purr : cat : :
   a. whale : wail
   b. lion : lioness
   c. rooster : farm
   d. bleat : sheep

3. colony : ants : :
   a. swarm : bees
   b. zebras : stripes
   c. bears : bares
   d. hogs : hive

4. kitten : cat : :
   a. otter : kit
   b. giraffe : colt
   c. cub : lion
   d. goat : fawn

5. bird : chirp : :
   a. bark : tree
   b. cow : moo
   c. croak : lizard
   d. meow : cry

6. chick : ostrich : :
   a. elephant : whelp
   b. tiger : lion
   c. kid : goat
   d. wolf : calf

7. tail : tale : :
   a. mammal : hair
   b. herd : elephant
   c. ewe : you
   d. filly : mare

8. lamb : sheep : :
   a. foal : foul
   b. rabbit : pup
   c. bird : eagle
   d. fawn : deer

9. hive : bee : :
   a. walrus : tusk
   b. den : lion
   c. coyote : desert
   d. bird : fly

10. pack : dogs : :
    a. herd : cattle
    b. pig : piglet
    c. hawk : bird
    d. turkey : poultry

21

Name_____

People

Instructions: Underline the word that best completes each analogy.
On the Answer Sheet, fill in the bubbles that match your answers.

1. actor : actress :: waiter :
   a. food
   b. server
   c. waitress
   d. chef

2. school : teacher :: laboratory :
   a. scientist
   b. experiment
   c. dancer
   d. pilot

3. plow : farmer :: stethoscope :
   a. lawyer
   b. doctor
   c. plumber
   d. astronomer

4. robber : thief :: journalist :
   a. column
   b. computer
   c. newspaper
   d. writer

5. composer : music :: architect :
   a. buildings
   b. electricity
   c. animals
   d. flowers

6. maid : made :: knight :
   a. kingdom
   b. night
   c. day
   d. armor

7. woman : women :: child :
   a. baby
   b. kid
   c. childs
   d. children

8. referee : basketball :: umpire :
   a. catcher
   b. football
   c. baseball
   d. sports

9. librarian : books :: botanist :
   a. stars
   b. birds
   c. rocks
   d. plants

10. nurse : hospital :: secretary :
    a. computer
    b. telephone
    c. office
    d. principal

Name_____

Sports

Instructions: Underline the word that best completes each analogy.
On the Answer Sheet, fill in the bubbles that match your answers.

1. pedal : bike : :
   a. baseball : football
   b. throw : toss
   c. row : boat
   d. dribble : catch

2. goal : soccer : :
   a. wrestling : mat
   b. strike : judo
   c. golf : course
   d. touchdown : football

3. win : lose : :
   a. stale : fresh
   b. score : number
   c. fierce : ferocious
   d. danger : peril

4. racket : tennis : :
   a. ball : net
   b. court : alley
   c. club : golf
   d. basketball : softball

5. boll : bowl : :
   a. team : player
   b. sport : race
   c. athlete : squad
   d. ball : bawl

6. hockey : ice : :
   a. yield : field
   b. soccer : grass
   c. canoe : boat
   d. glider : raft

7. swim : pool : :
   a. bowl : lane
   b. bike : pedal
   c. goal : score
   d. track : field

8. amateur : pro : :
   a. trophy : prize
   b. allow : forbid
   c. stadium : arena
   d. paddle : net

9. run : race : :
   a. play : game
   b. box : wrestle
   c. bike : row
   d. relay : sport

10. offense : defense : :
    a. joy : happiness
    b. advance : retreat
    c. often : frequent
    d. divulge : disclose

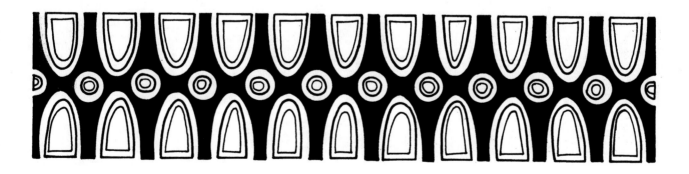

Analogy Challenge
© The Learning Works, Inc.

Name_____

Numbers and Measurement

Instructions: Underline the word that best completes each analogy.
On the Answer Sheet, fill in the bubbles that match your answers.

1. solo : one : : duet :
   a. music
   b. three
   c. two
   d. six

2. four : for : : eight :
   a. ate
   b. number
   c. dozen
   d. fraction

3. dozen : twelve : : trio :
   a. six
   b. song
   c. ten
   d. three

4. minute : hour : : day :
   a. night
   b. week
   c. second
   d. pound

5. even : odd : : addition :
   a. number
   b. sum
   c. subtraction
   d. division

6. tablespoon : teaspoon : : cup :
   a. glass
   b. yard
   c. inch
   d. ounce

7. second : minute : : month :
   a. calendar
   b. year
   c. hour
   d. decade

8. decade : ten : : century :
   a. fifty
   b. twenty
   c. hundred
   d. thousand

9. nickel : five : : dime :
   a. one
   b. cents
   c. ten
   d. coin

10. clock : time : : scale :
    a. vegetables
    b. balance
    c. distance
    d. weight

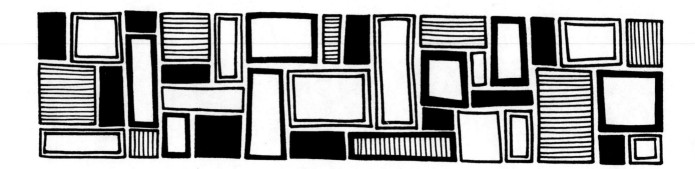

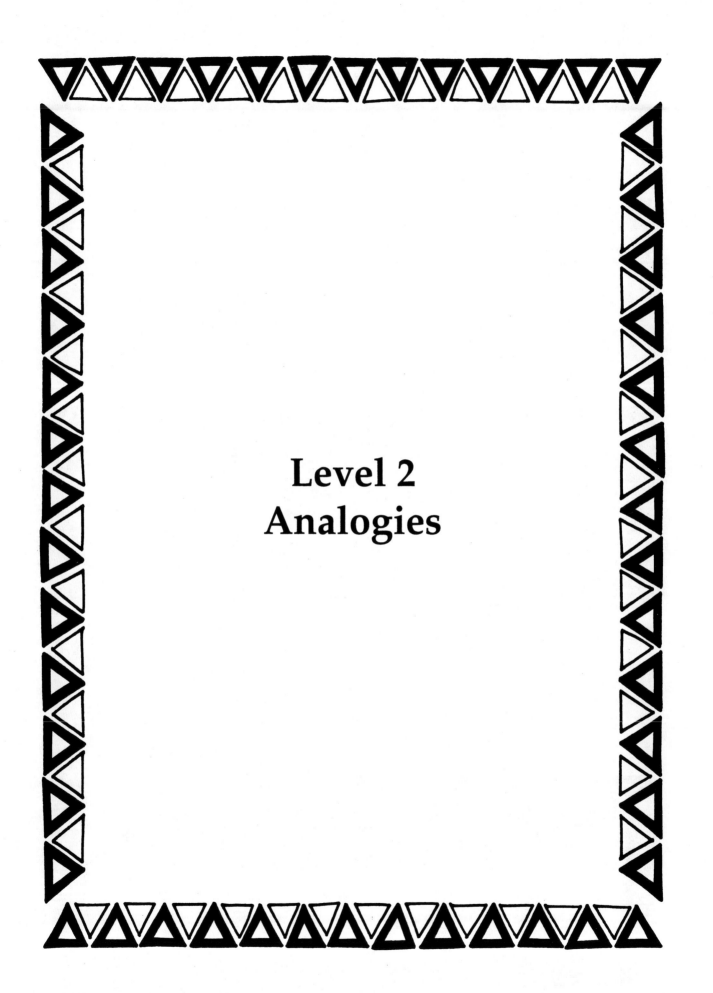

Level 2
Analogies

Name_____

Nouns

Instructions: Underline the word that best completes each analogy.
On the Answer Sheet, fill in the bubbles that match your answers.

1. loafers : shoe : : cardigan :
   a. sweater
   b. wool
   c. ascot
   d. skirt

2. cello : string : : flute :
   a. percussion
   b. woodwind
   c. music
   d. piccolo

3. promise : pledge : : peril :
   a. honesty
   b. pleasure
   c. beauty
   d. danger

4. corral : pen : : carriage :
   a. horse
   b. farm
   c. buggy
   d. wheelbarrow

5. worth : value : : exhibit :
   a. display
   b. theater
   c. movie
   d. convention

6. encyclopedia : book : : diamond :
   a. ruby
   b. baseball
   c. circle
   d. gem

7. jurisdiction : power : : rival :
   a. companion
   b. revival
   c. competitor
   d. contest

8. quarts : quartz : : reign :
   a. rule
   b. kingdom
   c. control
   d. rain

9. wrath : anger : : pallor :
   a. paleness
   b. parlor
   c. gloom
   d. shade

10. shrew : animal : : oriole :
    a. fish
    b. bird
    c. flower
    d. tree

Name_____

Verbs

Instructions: Underline the word that best completes each analogy.
On the Answer Sheet, fill in the bubbles that match your answers.

1. babble : chatter : : pulsate :
   a. speck
   b. throb
   c. steal
   d. attempt

2. magnify : intensify : : idolize :
   a. abhor
   b. despise
   c. abide
   d. adore

3. plentiful : abundant : : disclose :
   a. divulge
   b. overlook
   c. cease
   d. dilute

4. bawl : laugh : : humiliate :
   a. praise
   b. hide
   c. moisten
   d. shame

5. need : knead : : cite :
   a. quote
   b. mention
   c. sight
   d. manifest

6. separate : disconnect : : abandon :
   a. dessert
   b. alight
   c. confer
   d. desert

7. question : answer : : dwindle :
   a. glow
   b. shrink
   c. expand
   d. explode

8. decline : refuse : : stifle :
   a. begin
   b. suppress
   c. beat
   d. sniff

9. reflect : think : : reduce :
   a. lessen
   b. refine
   c. rebound
   d. retire

10. smother : suffocate : : pardon :
    a. please
    b. preach
    c. pry
    d. forgive

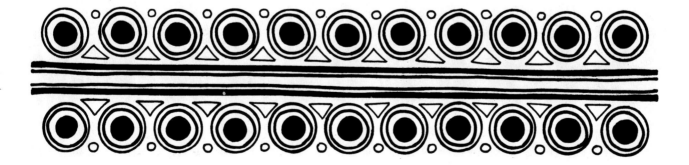

27

Analogy Challenge
© The Learning Works, Inc.

Adjectives

Instructions: Underline the word that best completes each analogy.
On the Answer Sheet, fill in the bubbles that match your answers.

1. precise : exact : : gaunt :
   a. secluded
   b. thin
   c. obtuse
   d. blunt

2. gnarled : twisted : : punctual :
   a. tardy
   b. plain
   c. prompt
   d. soft

3. limp : slack : : nimble :
   a. clumsy
   b. slow
   c. agile
   d. dark

4. dubious : doubtful : : catastrophic :
   a. disastrous
   b. catatonic
   c. supreme
   d. confident

5. disheveled : disorderly : : benevolent :
   a. obtuse
   b. agreeable
   c. charitable
   d. lifeless

6. luminous : dull : : jovial :
   a. immature
   b. sullen
   c. jolly
   d. jubilant

7. necessary : essential : : eerie :
   a. spooky
   b. eternal
   c. serene
   d. gorgeous

8. obvious : apparent : : petty :
   a. tiny
   b. previous
   c. trivial
   d. plain

9. covert : open : : obscure :
   a. fuzzy
   b. obsolete
   c. hidden
   d. distinct

10. feeble : robust : : zealous :
    a. jealous
    b. lonely
    c. unenthusiastic
    d. lively

Name_____

Adverbs

Instructions: Underline the word that best completes each analogy.
On the Answer Sheet, fill in the bubbles that match your answers.

1. idly : busily : : politely :
   a. popularly
   b. preciously
   c. radically
   d. rudely

2. obviously : apparently : : severely :
   a. harshly
   b. openly
   c. cautiously
   d. hardly

3. innocently : guiltily : : passively :
   a. calmly
   b. actively
   c. quietly
   d. compactly

4. cheerfully : somberly : : daintily :
   a. fondly
   b. deviously
   c. clumsily
   d. devoutly

5. peacefully : tranquilly : : meekly :
   a. overly
   b. excitedly
   c. mildly
   d. lonely

6. abruptly : suddenly : : coarsely :
   a. smoothly
   b. roughly
   c. calmly
   d. finely

7. moistly : damply : : frequently :
   a. dejectedly
   b. densely
   c. fully
   d. often

8. inwardly : outwardly : : restlessly :
   a. nervously
   b. calmly
   c. candidly
   d. slowly

9. perfectly : flawlessly : : prominently :
   a. secretly
   b. actually
   c. noticeably
   d. narrowly

10. legally : illegally : : partly :
    a. completely
    b. partially
    c. particularly
    d. crazily

29

Analogy Challenge
© The Learning Works, Inc.

Name_____

Review of Parts of Speech

Instructions: Underline the word that best completes each analogy.
On the Answer Sheet, fill in the bubbles that match your answers.

1. crimson : red : : indigo :
   a. green
   b. purple
   c. black
   d. blue

2. investigate : explore : : prolong :
   a. extend
   b. shorten
   c. preview
   d. decide

3. femur : leg : : scapula :
   a. skull
   b. shoulder
   c. scalp
   d. spatula

4. suggestion : implication : : importance :
   a. intellect
   b. intention
   c. consequence
   d. significance

5. scare : frighten : : mediocre :
   a. outstanding
   b. soothing
   c. ordinary
   d. brave

6. tease : taunt : : trivial :
   a. important
   b. outstanding
   c. pretty
   d. petty

7. mackerel : fish : : emu :
   a. reptile
   b. bird
   c. mammal
   d. trout

8. sun : star : : Earth :
   a. satellite
   b. meteor
   c. moon
   d. planet

9. flag : pole : : sail :
   a. mast
   b. sale
   c. cloth
   d. flag

10. joke : trick : : caper :
    a. cloak
    b. riddle
    c. prank
    d. appetizer

Name_____

Synonyms

Instructions: Underline the word that best completes each analogy.
On the Answer Sheet, fill in the bubbles that match your answers.

1. probe : explore : : intimidate :
   a. infer
   b. hide
   c. signal
   d. frighten

2. sparse : meager : : cognizant :
   a. insensitive
   b. aware
   c. defective
   d. elegant

3. route : course : : frivolous :
   a. silly
   b. favorite
   c. necessary
   d. important

4. courage : bravery : : mediocre :
   a. corpulent
   b. spicy
   c. average
   d. poor

5. prior : previous : : prolong :
   a. provide
   b. extend
   c. oblong
   d. protect

6. scold : reprimand : : persevere :
   a. linger
   b. hoist
   c. disregard
   d. persist

7. feeble : decrepit : : coagulate :
   a. regulate
   b. congeal
   c. coast
   d. conspire

8. fret : worry : : trait :
   a. characteristic
   b. trade
   c. transformation
   d. doubt

9. assemble : gather : : conjecture :
   a. guide
   b. steal
   c. guess
   d. grab

10. alike : identical : : tranquil :
    a. timid
    b. devious
    c. peaceful
    d. hardy

31

Analogy Challenge
© The Learning Works, Inc.

Name_____

Antonyms

Instructions: Underline the word that best completes each analogy.
On the Answer Sheet, fill in the bubbles that match your answers.

1. simple : complex : : synthetic :
    a. sincere
    b. lonesome
    c. hearty
    d. natural

2. aloof : familiar : : raze :
    a. demolish
    b. destroy
    c. construct
    d. dazzle

3. constrict : dilate : : inertia :
    a. intimate
    b. energy
    c. idleness
    d. interval

4. appear : vanish : : abate :
    a. increase
    b. rebate
    c. doubt
    d. omit

5. antiquated : modern : : cognizant :
    a. dormant
    b. irregular
    c. ignorant
    d. conceit

6. include : omit : : trite :
    a. tiny
    b. original
    c. stale
    d. sharp

7. positive : negative : : commence :
    a. transact
    b. accept
    c. hasten
    d. conclude

8. optimistic : pessimistic : : melancholy :
    a. jovial
    b. melodious
    c. lonely
    d. finicky

9. compliment : criticize : : spurn :
    a. refuse
    b. spin
    c. accept
    d. clear

10. rejection : acceptance : : inclement :
    a. attentive
    b. dangerous
    c. mild
    d. sharp

Name_____

Review of Synonyms and Antonyms

Instructions: Underline the word that best completes each analogy.
On the Answer Sheet, fill in the bubbles that match your answers.

1. hasten : delay : : scant :
   a. scent
   b. meager
   c. abundant
   d. skimpy

2. obstacle : obstruction : : zeal :
   a. enthusiasm
   b. animal
   c. reform
   d. loneliness

3. interrogate : question : : lure :
   a. entice
   b. look
   c. climb
   d. investigate

4. cruel : kind : : latter :
   a. previous
   b. former
   c. third
   d. last

5. sustain : support : : influence :
   a. reap
   b. isolate
   c. sway
   d. infect

6. increase : decrease : : believe :
   a. think
   b. trust
   c. depend
   d. doubt

7. heedless : careful : : rare :
   a. steak
   b. common
   c. unusual
   d. shallow

8. danger : peril : : obvious :
   a. reasonable
   b. difficult
   c. hidden
   d. apparent

9. nimble : spry : : snug :
   a. loose
   b. tight
   c. harsh
   d. moist

10. exact : vague : : ambitious :
    a. absent
    b. trustworthy
    c. lazy
    d. coy

33

Name_____

Food

Instructions: Underline the word that best completes each analogy.
On the Answer Sheet, fill in the bubbles that match your answers.

1. knead : dough : : whip :
   a. beat
   b. cream
   c. strap
   d. beef

2. beef : cow : : poultry :
   a. chicken
   b. fish
   c. pork
   d. bull

3. cheese : milk : : ketchup :
   a. red
   b. mustard
   c. hamburger
   d. tomato

4. broccoli : vegetable : : kiwi :
   a. green
   b. cauliflower
   c. beverage
   d. fruit

5. yolk : yoke : : steak :
   a. meat
   b. sirloin
   c. stake
   d. dinner

6. halibut : fish : : squab :
   a. bird
   b. chicken
   c. venison
   d. deer

7. loaf : bread : : head :
   a. bananas
   b. lettuce
   c. potatoes
   d. onions

8. bake : pie : : poach :
   a. candy
   b. carrot
   c. pea
   d. egg

9. whip : beat : : mince :
   a. pie
   b. cut
   c. sauté
   d. fry

10. skin : peach : : shell :
    a. banana
    b. apple
    c. okra
    d. egg

Name_____

Animals

Instructions: Underline the word that best completes each analogy.
On the Answer Sheet, fill in the bubbles that match your answers.

1. beak : bird : : antenna :
   a. fish
   b. reptile
   c. insect
   d. cat

2. canine : dog : : feline :
   a. hog
   b. filly
   c. fish
   d. cat

3. kid : antelope : : gosling :
   a. eel
   b. goose
   c. goat
   d. giraffe

4. antler : deer : : horn :
   a. hippopotamus
   b. penguin
   c. tiger
   d. deer

5. wolf : wolves : : moose :
   a. mooses
   b. muster
   c. moose
   d. meese

6. cow : bull : : mare :
   a. colt
   b. stallion
   c. pony
   d. filly

7. pod : whales : : gaggle :
   a. geese
   b. pheasants
   c. monkeys
   d. rabbits

8. calf : rhinoceros : : colt :
   a. tiger
   b. cat
   c. duck
   d. zebra

9. beetle : insect : : piranha :
   a. mammal
   b. reptile
   c. fish
   d. bird

10. pride : lion : : colony :
    a. cat
    b. kangaroo
    c. rabbit
    d. cow

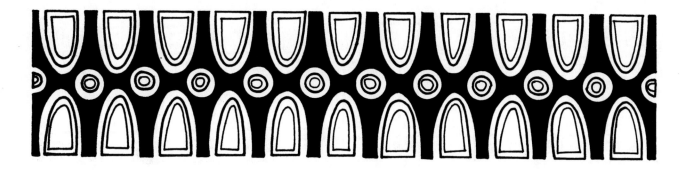

Analogy Challenge
© The Learning Works, Inc.

Name_____

People

Instructions: Underline the word that best completes each analogy.
On the Answer Sheet, fill in the bubbles that match your answers.

1. aunt : uncle : : niece :
   a. sister
   b. daughter
   c. nephew
   d. brother

2. gardener : rake : : carpenter :
   a. hammer
   b. house
   c. builder
   d. tongs

3. doctor : hospital : : photographer :
   a. pictures
   b. studio
   c. camera
   d. tripod

4. pilot : airplane : : astronaut :
   a. weightlessness
   b. spacecraft
   c. automobile
   d. cosmonaut

5. pharmacist : druggist : : magician
   a. mechanic
   b. mathematician
   c. tyrant
   d. sorcerer

6. leader : group : : captain :
   a. king
   b. ruler
   c. chief
   d. crew

7. brush : artist : : baton :
   a. stick
   b. philosopher
   c. conductor
   d. parade

8. player : team : : actress :
   a. actor
   b. stage
   c. cast
   d. theater

9. student : classroom : : witness :
   a. jury
   b. courtroom
   c. judge
   d. lawyer

10. florist : flowers : : geologist :
    a. numbers
    b. animals
    c. rocks
    d. stars

Name_____

Sports

Instructions: Underline the word that best completes each analogy.
On the Answer Sheet, fill in the bubbles that match your answers.

1. defeat : triumph : : pursue :
   a. achieve
   b. avoid
   c. advance
   d. attempt

2. birdie : badminton : : puck :
   a. ice
   b. shuttlecock
   c. hockey
   d. shuffleboard

3. hoop : basketball : : wicket :
   a. baseball
   b. score
   c. field
   d. cricket

4. backhand : tennis : : breaststroke :
   a. dancing
   b. racket
   c. swimming
   d. freestyle

5. bunt : punt : : field :
   a. throw
   b. yield
   c. grass
   d. ball

6. bull's eye : archery : : knockout :
   a. boxing
   b. wrestling
   c. bowling
   d. tennis

7. canter : gallop : : creep :
   a. paddock
   b. rush
   c. slide
   d. horse

8. pitch : lob : : toss :
   a. fumble
   b. ball
   c. throw
   d. catch

9. slalom : skiing : : dressage :
   a. riding
   b. jockey
   c. downhill
   d. skating

10. referee : officiate : : commentator :
    a. coach
    b. correct
    c. instruct
    d. discuss

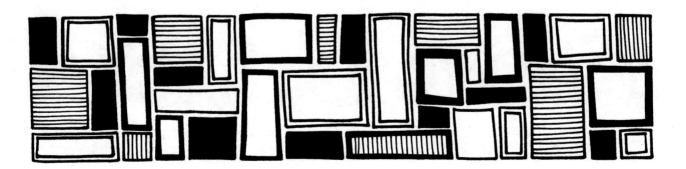

37

Analogy Challenge
© The Learning Works, Inc.

Name_____

Numbers and Measurement

Instructions: Underline the word that best completes each analogy.
On the Answer Sheet, fill in the bubbles that match your answers.

1. ten : decade : : thousand :
   a. million
   b. year
   c. century
   d. millennium

2. bushel : peck : : minute :
   a. week
   b. rod
   c. clock
   d. second

3. pound : ton : : pint :
   a. acre
   b. tablespoon
   c. quart
   d. inch

4. four : quartet : : eight :
   a. octet
   b. whole
   c. ate
   d. quarter

5. triangle : three : : pentagon :
   a. seven
   b. four
   c. six
   d. five

6. day : week : : month :
   a. hour
   b. year
   c. second
   d. minute

7. ruler : inches : : thermometer :
   a. temperature
   b. flu
   c. rain
   d. pound

8. century : hundred : : score :
   a. five
   b. ten
   c. twenty
   d. fifty

9. compass : circle : : protractor :
   a. course
   b. angle
   c. parallel
   d. ruler

10. yard : inch : : meter :
    a. metrics
    b. foot
    c. ton
    d. centimeter

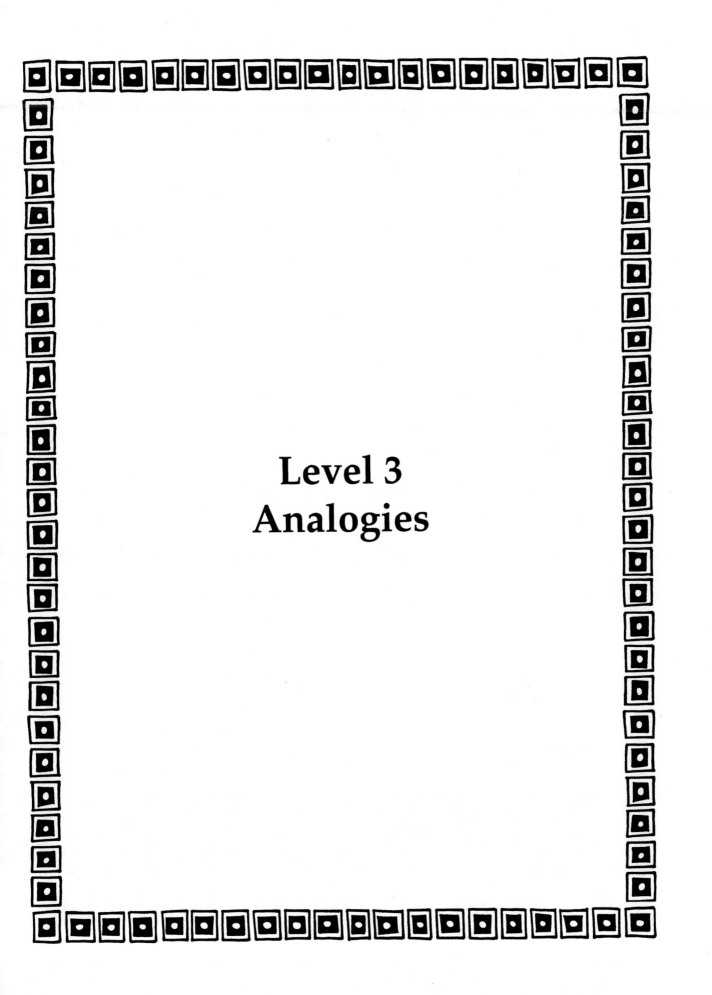

Level 3
Analogies

Nouns

Instructions: Underline the word that best completes each analogy.
On the Answer Sheet, fill in the bubbles that match your answers.

1. cactus : cactuses : : larva :
   a. larvi
   b. larvas
   c. larvases
   d. larvae

2. pinnacle : peak : : domicile :
   a. residence
   b. dome
   c. hallway
   d. doorman

3. piccolo : woodwind : : trombone :
   a. percussion
   b. string
   c. brass
   d. trumpet

4. cirrus : cloud : : viola :
   a. violet
   b. flower
   c. vessel
   d. instrument

5. botany : plants : : hydrology :
   a. blood
   b. water
   c. minerals
   d. heat

6. appendicitis : appendix : : hepatitis :
   a. liver
   b. kidney
   c. heart
   d. nerve

7. deficiency : inadequacy : : zenith :
   a. perigee
   b. mountain
   c. summit
   d. zero

8. zealot : fanatic : : avocation :
   a. airplane
   b. benediction
   c. vacation
   d. hobby

9. blemish : flaw : : innuendo :
   a. insinuation
   b. inoculation
   c. inquiry
   d. inscription

10. aspen : tree : : narcissus :
    a. fish
    b. mineral
    c. rock
    d. flower

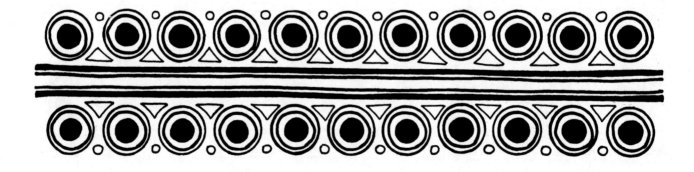

Name_____

Verbs

Instructions: Underline the word that best completes each analogy.
On the Answer Sheet, fill in the bubbles that match your answers.

1. extinguish : ignite : : convene :
   a. meet
   b. disperse
   c. convert
   d. congregate

2. embrace : spurn : : enunciate :
   a. articulate
   b. mumble
   c. pronounce
   d. proclaim

3. reject : repulse : : reiterate :
   a. reinvest
   b. relate
   c. relapse
   d. repeat

4. slander : defame : : flit :
   a. dart
   b. ignite
   c. flirt
   d. stick

5. squander : waste : : condone :
   a. complete
   b. pardon
   c. disapprove
   d. disappear

6. submit : resist : : debilitate :
   a. divide
   b. ruin
   c. defraud
   d. invigorate

7. initiate : commence : : interrogate :
   a. intervene
   b. intend
   c. question
   d. arrest

8. hasten : delay : : placate :
   a. place
   b. enrage
   c. manifest
   d. restrict

9. mock : ridicule : : evoke :
   a. elicit
   b. return
   c. engage
   d. eject

10. guarantee : ensure : : entice :
    a. empty
    b. elect
    c. divert
    d. lure

41

Adjectives

Instructions: Underline the word that best completes each analogy.
On the Answer Sheet, fill in the bubbles that match your answers.

1. opulent : wealthy : : loquacious :
   a. absurd
   b. versatile
   c. talkative
   d. jubilant

2. gawky : graceful : : scrupulous :
   a. massive
   b. delightful
   c. faithful
   d. unethical

3. nebulous : clear : : frivolous :
   a. silly
   b. frugal
   c. serious
   d. flippant

4. haughty : arrogant : : explicit :
   a. difficult
   b. definite
   c. prolonged
   d. uncertain

5. somnolent : drowsy : : plethora :
   a. excess
   b. plump
   c. shear
   d. prosperous

6. malodorous : fragrant : : transitory :
   a. amenable
   b. apathetic
   c. perpetual
   d. limber

7. lethargic : energetic : : impudent :
   a. polite
   b. immature
   c. argumentative
   d. rude

8. murky : muddy : : ominous :
   a. callow
   b. tranquil
   c. threatening
   d. ordinary

9. vivacious : lively : : succinct :
   a. obstinate
   b. smelly
   c. prominent
   d. concise

10. mediocre : average : : mendacious :
    a. redundant
    b. dishonest
    c. scrupulous
    d. venerable

Name_____

Adverbs

Instructions: Underline the word that best completes each analogy.
On the Answer Sheet, fill in the bubbles that match your answers.

1. fondly : affectionately : : hastily :
   a. slowly
   b. hauntingly
   c. hurriedly
   d. haphazardly

2. intentionally : purposely : : zestfully :
   a. sadly
   b. enthusiastically
   c. interestingly
   d. openly

3. nervously : calmly : : zealously :
   a. passionately
   b. earnestly
   c. seriously
   d. apathetically

4. humbly : insignificantly : : hypocritically :
   a. insincerely
   b. immediately
   c. jealously
   d. plainly

5. slovenly : disorderly : : cunningly :
   a. honestly
   b. slyly
   c. sweetly
   d. bitterly

6. justifiably : excusably : : auspiciously :
   a. awkwardly
   b. avidly
   c. barely
   d. favorably

7. crazily : sanely : : indecisively :
   a. immediately
   b. curtly
   c. conclusively
   d. independently

8. wobbly : shaky : : tenaciously :
   a. strongly
   b. tentatively
   c. occasionally
   d. weakly

9. precisely : exactly : : desolately :
   a. desperately
   b. deplorably
   c. happily
   d. gloomily

10. completely : thoroughly : : obnoxiously :
    a. openly
    b. obliviously
    c. onerously
    d. repugnantly

Analogy Challenge
© The Learning Works, Inc.

Name_____

Review of Parts of Speech

Instructions: Underline the word that best completes each analogy.
On the Answer Sheet, fill in the bubbles that match your answers.

1. russet : brown : : azure :
   a. color
   b. khaki
   c. blue
   d. green

2. poplar : tree : : gneiss :
   a. rock
   b. animal
   c. flower
   d. disease

3. hamper : clothes : : canteen :
   a. pitcher
   b. vase
   c. water
   d. desert

4. corrode : erode : : mirth :
   a. tedium
   b. glee
   c. sadness
   d. mischief

5. zebu : mammal : : kea :
   a. fish
   b. flower
   c. reptile
   d. bird

6. exterior : interior : : solicitous :
   a. solitary
   b. negligent
   c. flimsy
   d. temporary

7. squeamish : queasy : : florid :
   a. frequent
   b. pale
   c. fluffy
   d. ruddy

8. zenith : nadir : : subservient :
   a. menial
   b. obsequious
   c. authorative
   d. sensitive

9. violently : extremely : : sporadically :
   a. infrequently
   b. smoothly
   c. luxuriously
   d. miraculously

10. ravenous : voracious : : portentous :
    a. popular
    b. ominous
    c. outrageous
    d. possessive

Name_____

Synonyms

Instructions: Underline the word that best completes each analogy.
On the Answer Sheet, fill in the bubbles that match your answers.

1. innocuous : harmless : : insipid :
   a. dull
   b. tasty
   c. exciting
   d. inside

2. enclose : confine : : concoct :
   a. control
   b. direct
   c. approve
   d. devise

3. lucrative : profitable : : impetuous :
   a. analogous
   b. stubborn
   c. impulsive
   d. repulsive

4. irate : angry : : ennui :
   a. excitement
   b. boredom
   c. jealousy
   d. wealthy

5. contemporary : modern : : ubiquitous :
   a. widespread
   b. courteous
   c. unique
   d. adroit

6. shrink : recoil : : placate :
   a. enrage
   b. pacify
   c. pity
   d. scheme

7. arrogant : haughty : : tawdry :
   a. squeamish
   b. tricky
   c. strident
   d. showy

8. repose : lie : : repudiate :
   a. tattle
   b. quarrel
   c. repeat
   d. decline

9. wreak : cause : : aberrant :
   a. abnormal
   b. plague
   c. chivalry
   d. compulsion

10. disastrous : catastrophic : : erudite :
    a. shocking
    b. abruptly
    c. scholarly
    d. nebulous

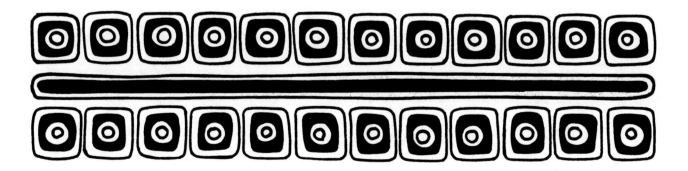

Analogy Challenge
© The Learning Works, Inc.

Name_____

Antonyms

Instructions: Underline the word that best completes each analogy.
On the Answer Sheet, fill in the bubbles that match your answers.

1. comply : resist : : descent :
   a. deserve
   b. decent
   c. assert
   d. ascent

2. lithe : rigid : : rescind :
   a. repeat
   b. renew
   c. withdraw
   d. remind

3. impair : improve : : mollify :
   a. calm
   b. penetrate
   c. manifest
   d. exasperate

4. assume : abdicate : : extol :
   a. praise
   b. extend
   c. shorten
   d. criticize

5. diurnal : nocturnal : : scrupulous :
   a. remiss
   b. malevolent
   c. fastidious
   d. careful

6. repulsive : attractive : : sanguine :
   a. sweet
   b. cheerful
   c. sanitary
   d. pessimistic

7. copious : meager : : pusillanimous :
   a. courageous
   b. pushy
   c. infectious
   d. contemptuous

8. recalcitrant : amenable : : facile :
   a. apathetic
   b. effortless
   c. arduous
   d. tranquil

9. articulate : unintelligible : : zenith :
   a. apogee
   b. zephyr
   c. nadir
   d. reciprocal

10. proficiency : incompetence : : vindicate :
    a. pardon
    b. spurn
    c. neglect
    d. accuse

Name_____

Review of Synonyms and Antonyms

Instructions: Underline the word that best completes each analogy.
On the Answer Sheet, fill in the bubbles that match your answers.

1. waste : squander : : pummel :
   a. beat
   b. purchase
   c. prove
   d. promote

2. physician : doctor : : replica :
   a. request
   b. reminder
   c. copy
   d. recommendation

3. ponder : meditate : : vacillate :
   a. worry
   b. inoculate
   c. verify
   d. waiver

4. dullness : luminance : : guile :
   a. estimate
   b. guess
   c. cunning
   d. candor

5. silent : loquacious : : laudable :
   a. laughable
   b. abominable
   c. praiseworthy
   d. commendable

6. outrageous : heinous : : impulsive :
   a. plodding
   b. thoughtful
   c. inquisitive
   d. spontaneous

7. impudent : respectful : : domineering :
   a. demanding
   b. powerful
   c. subservient
   d. foolish

8. somnolent : drowsy : : pompous :
   a. timid
   b. arrogant
   c. popular
   d. prejudice

9. lavish : luxuriant : : oblivious :
   a. obvious
   b. knowledgeable
   c. innocent
   d. forgetful

10. sagacious : shrewd : : vindictive :
    a. spiteful
    b. beneficial
    c. benevolent
    d. victorious

Analogy Challenge
© The Learning Works, Inc.

Name_____

Food

Instructions: Underline the word that best completes each analogy.
On the Answer Sheet, fill in the bubbles that match your answers.

1. pippin : apple : : leek :
   a. leak
   b. onion
   c. fruit
   d. pepper

2. flan : dessert : : vichyssoise :
   a. salad
   b. bread
   c. soup
   d. drink

3. kumquat : fruit : : escargot :
   a. snail
   b. potato
   c. tofu
   d. steak

4. bland : dull : : truss :
   a. clean
   b. wash
   c. scrape
   d. bind

5. bouillon : soup : : endive :
   a. salad
   b. drink
   c. pasta
   d. dessert

6. bucket : ice : : pitcher :
   a. mug
   b. baseball
   c. fruit
   d. tea

7. navel : orange : : casaba :
   a. melon
   b. lettuce
   c. squash
   d. vegetable

8. rutabaga : vegetable : : gherkin :
   a. dessert
   b. nut
   c. pickle
   d. pudding

9. scramble : egg : : mash :
   a. crush
   b. dice
   c. bread
   d. potato

10. iceberg : lettuce : : yam :
    a. cauliflower
    b. potato
    c. tomato
    d. grapefruit

Name_____

Animals

Instructions: Underline the word that best completes each analogy.
On the Answer Sheet, fill in the bubbles that match your answers.

1. beagle : dog : : manx :
   a. cat
   b. monkey
   c. amphibian
   d. mongoose

2. eaglet : eagle : : joey :
   a. donkey
   b. jaguar
   c. bobcat
   d. kangaroo

3. wombat : mammal : : kestrel :
   a. fish
   b. reptile
   c. insect
   d. bird

4. sardine : fish : : ibex :
   a. insect
   b. fish
   c. mammal
   d. bird

5. reptiles : herpetology : : insects :
   a. entomology
   b. geology
   c. ichthyology
   d. zoology

6. emu : bird : : sturgeon :
   a. dog
   b. lizard
   c. fish
   d. dinosaur

7. whelp : seal : : cygnet :
   a. swan
   b. giraffe
   c. duck
   d. eagle

8. rooster : chicken : : drake :
   a. pigeon
   b. duck
   c. ewe
   d. cat

9. zoology : animals : : ornithology :
   a. worms
   b. whales
   c. mollusks
   d. birds

10. gerbil : mammal : : anaconda :
    a. insect
    b. snake
    c. fish
    d. bird

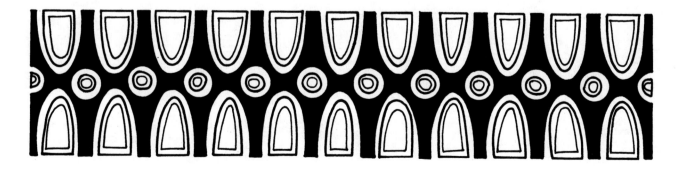

Analogy Challenge
© The Learning Works, Inc.

People

Instructions: Underline the word that best completes each analogy.
On the Answer Sheet, fill in the bubbles that match your answers.

1. heroine : hero : : aviatrix :
   a. plane
   b. aviator
   c. pilot
   d. flight

2. criminologist : crime : : meteorologist :
   a. flowers
   b. asteroids
   c. meteors
   d. weather

3. hermit : recluse : : miner :
   a. prospector
   b. explorer
   c. astronaut
   d. minor

4. podiatrist : feet : : cardiologist :
   a. cards
   b. heart
   c. kidneys
   d. liver

5. sleuth : investigator : : negotiate :
   a. convert
   b. retaliate
   c. negate
   d. bargain

6. courier : messenger : : philanthropist :
   a. miser
   b. benefactor
   c. musician
   d. orchestra

7. dermatologist : skin : : hematologist :
   a. reptiles
   b. glands
   c. blood
   d. brain

8. emigrant : immigrant : : optimist :
   a. entrepreneur
   b. optometrist
   c. podiatrist
   d. pessimist

9. lithographer : prints : : cartographer :
   a. cartoons
   b. carts
   c. rocks
   d. maps

10. conchologist : shells : : numismatist :
    a. coins
    b. numbers
    c. fossils
    d. skulls

Numbers and Measurement

Instructions: Underline the word that best completes each analogy.
On the Answer Sheet, fill in the bubbles that match your answers.

1. feet : altitude : : fathom :
   a. liquid
   b. depth
   c. furlong
   d. yard

2. velocity : speed : : capacity :
   a. volume
   b. width
   c. height
   d. emptiness

3. acre : land : : decibel :
   a. sound
   b. space
   c. electricity
   d. current

4. hexagon : six : : heptagon :
   a. five
   b. twenty
   c. seven
   d. ten

5. finite : unlimited : : immense :
   a. extreme
   b. expanse
   c. enormous
   d. diminutive

6. decimeter : length : : gram :
   a. yardstick
   b. liquid
   c. capacity
   d. weight

7. barometer : pressure : : odometer :
   a. depth
   b. miles
   c. time
   d. speed

8. inches : foot : : rod :
   a. furlong
   b. stick
   c. minute
   d. ton

9. factor : multiplication : : minuend :
   a. division
   b. subtraction
   c. addition
   d. fraction

10. peck : bushel : : quart :
    a. acre
    b. area
    c. gallon
    d. pint

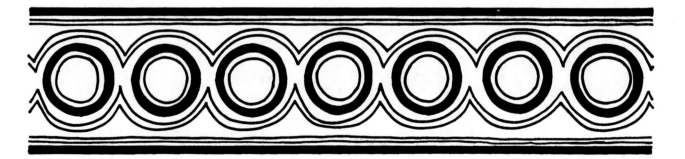

Analogy Challenge
© The Learning Works, Inc.

Answer Sheet

Student's Name _____

Activity _____ Level _____ Page No. _____

	a b c d		a b c d
1.	0000	6.	0000
2.	0000	7.	0000
3.	0000	8.	0000
4.	0000	9.	0000
5.	0000	10.	0000

Answer Sheet

Student's Name _____

Activity _____ Level _____ Page No. _____

	a b c d		a b c d
1.	0000	6.	0000
2.	0000	7.	0000
3.	0000	8.	0000
4.	0000	9.	0000
5.	0000	10.	0000

Answer Sheet

Student's Name _____

Activity _____ Level _____ Page No. _____

	a b c d		a b c d
1.	0000	6.	0000
2.	0000	7.	0000
3.	0000	8.	0000
4.	0000	9.	0000
5.	0000	10.	0000

Create Your Own Analogies

Now that you have had practice in completing analogies, try creating some of your own. Use a dictionary, thesaurus, or similar reference materials to create your analogies

Analogies Based on Synonyms or Antonyms

1. _____ : _____ :: _____ : _____
2. _____ : _____ :: _____ : _____
3. _____ : _____ :: _____ : _____
4. _____ : _____ :: _____ : _____
5. _____ : _____ :: _____ : _____
6. _____ : _____ :: _____ : _____
7. _____ : _____ :: _____ : _____
8. _____ : _____ :: _____ : _____
9. _____ : _____ :: _____ : _____
10. _____ : _____ :: _____ : _____

Analogies Based on Verbs and Adverbs

1. _____ : _____ :: _____ : _____
2. _____ : _____ :: _____ : _____
3. _____ : _____ :: _____ : _____
4. _____ : _____ :: _____ : _____
5. _____ : _____ :: _____ : _____
6. _____ : _____ :: _____ : _____
7. _____ : _____ :: _____ : _____
8. _____ : _____ :: _____ : _____
9. _____ : _____ :: _____ : _____
10. _____ : _____ :: _____ : _____

Analogy Challenge
© The Learning Works, Inc.

Create Your Own Analogies

On the lines below, create analogies for classmates to complete. Use a dictionary, thesaurus, or similar reference materials to create your analogies

Analogies Based on Nouns and Adjectives

1. _____ : _____ :: _____ : _____
2. _____ : _____ :: _____ : _____
3. _____ : _____ :: _____ : _____
4. _____ : _____ :: _____ : _____
5. _____ : _____ :: _____ : _____
6. _____ : _____ :: _____ : _____
7. _____ : _____ :: _____ : _____
8. _____ : _____ :: _____ : _____
9. _____ : _____ :: _____ : _____
10. _____ : _____ :: _____ : _____

Analogies Based on Parts to a Whole, Animal Offspring, Colors, Male and Female Counterparts, or Tools Associated With Occupations

1. _____ : _____ :: _____ : _____
2. _____ : _____ :: _____ : _____
3. _____ : _____ :: _____ : _____
4. _____ : _____ :: _____ : _____
5. _____ : _____ :: _____ : _____
6. _____ : _____ :: _____ : _____
7. _____ : _____ :: _____ : _____
8. _____ : _____ :: _____ : _____
9. _____ : _____ :: _____ : _____
10. _____ : _____ :: _____ : _____

Answer Key

Page 9 • Analogy Practice
1. d   2. a   3. b   4 d
5. d   6. b   7. c

Page 10 • Analogy Practice
1. synonyms; c
2. antonyms; d

Level 1 Analogies

Page 12 • Nouns
1. d   6. c
2. a   7. d
3. d   8. b
4. c   9. d
5. a   10. c

Page 13 • Verbs
1. c   6. c
2. a   7. c
3. c   8. b
4. c   9. d
5. d   10. c

Page 14 • Adjectives
1. b   6. d
2. a   7. c
3. c   8. a
4. d   9. b
5. b   10. c

Page 15 • Adverbs
1. b   6. a
2. c   7. b
3. b   8. c
4. d   9. b
5. c   10. d

Page 16 • Review of Parts of Speech
1. d   6. d
2. a   7. d
3. c   8. b
4. b   9. a
5. c   10. c

Page 17 • Synonyms
1. c   6. c
2. a   7. a
3. c   8. c
4. d   9. b
5. b   10. d

Page 18 • Antonyms
1. c   6. d
2. b   7. a
3. b   8. c
4. d   9. b
5. c   10. d

Page 19 • Review of Synonyms and Antonyms
1. b   6. b
2. c   7. d
3. a   8. c
4. b   9. b
5. d   10. c

Page 20 • Food
1. c   6. b
2. d   7. c
3. a   8. b
4. c   9. d
5. a   10. b

Page 21 • Animals
1. b   6. c
2. d   7. c
3. a   8. d
4. c   9. b
5. b   10. a

Page 22 • People
1. c   6. b
2. a   7. d
3. b   8. c
4. d   9. d
5. a   10. c

Page 23 • Sports
1. c   6. b
2. d   7. a
3. a   8. b
4. c   9. a
5. d   10. b

Page 24 • Numbers and Measurement
1. c   6. d
2. a   7. b
3. d   8. c
4. b   9. c
5. c   10. d

Level 2 Analogies

Page 26 • Nouns
1. a   6. d
2. b   7. c
3. d   8. d
4. c   9. a
5. a   10. b

Page 27 • Verbs
1. b   6. d
2. d   7. c
3. a   8. b
4. a   9. a
5. c   10. d

Page 28 • Adjectives
1. b   6. b
2. c   7. a
3. c   8. c
4. a   9. d
5. c   10. c

Page 29 • Adverbs
1. d   6. b
2. a   7. d
3. b   8. b
4. c   9. c
5. c   10. a

Page 30 • Review of Parts of Speech
1. d   6. d
2. a   7. b
3. b   8. d
4. d   9. a
5. c   10. c

Page 31 • Synonyms
1. d   6. d
2. b   7. b
3. a   8. a
4. c   9. c
5. b   10. c

Page 32 • Antonyms
1. d   6. b
2. c   7. d
3. b   8. a
4. a   9. c
5. c   10. c

Answer Key

Page 33 • Review of Synonyms and Antonyms

1.	c	6.	d
2.	a	7.	b
3.	a	8.	d
4.	b	9.	b
5.	c	10.	c

Page 34 • Food

1.	b	6.	a
2.	a	7.	b
3.	d	8.	d
4.	d	9.	b
5.	c	10.	d

Page 35 • Animals

1.	c	6.	b
2.	d	7.	a
3.	b	8.	d
4.	d	9.	c
5.	c	10.	c

Page 36 • People

1.	c	6.	d
2.	a	7.	c
3.	b	8.	c
4.	b	9.	b
5.	d	10.	c

Page 37 • Sports

1.	b	6.	a
2.	c	7.	b
3.	d	8.	c
4.	c	9.	a
5.	b	10.	d

Page 38 • Numbers and Measurement

1.	d	6.	b
2.	d	7.	a
3.	c	8.	c
4.	a	9.	b
5.	d	10.	d

Level 3 Analogies

Page 40 • Nouns

1.	d	6.	a
2.	a	7.	c
3.	c	8.	d
4.	d	9.	a
5.	b	10.	d

Page 41 • Verbs

1.	b	6.	d
2.	b	7.	c
3.	d	8.	b
4.	a	9.	a
5.	b	10.	d

Page 42 • Adjectives

1.	c	6.	c
2.	d	7.	a
3.	c	8.	c
4.	b	9.	d
5.	a	10.	b

Page 43 • Adverbs

1.	c	6.	d
2.	b	7.	c
3.	d	8.	a
4.	a	9.	d
5.	b	10.	d

Page 44 • Review of Parts of Speech

1.	c	6.	b
2.	a	7.	d
3.	c	8.	c
4.	b	9.	a
5.	d	10.	b

Page 45 • Synonyms

1.	a	6.	b
2.	d	7.	d
3.	c	8.	d
4.	b	9.	a
5.	a	10.	c

Page 46 • Antonyms

1.	d	6.	b
2.	b	7.	a
3.	d	8.	c
4.	d	9.	c
5.	a	10.	d

Page 47 • Review of Synonyms and Antonyms

1.	a	6.	d
2.	c	7.	c
3.	d	8.	b
4.	d	9.	d
5.	b	10.	a

Page 48 • Food

1.	b	6.	d
2.	c	7.	a
3.	a	8.	c
4.	d	9.	d
5.	a	10.	b

Page 49 • Animals

1.	a	6.	c
2.	d	7.	a
3.	d	8.	b
4.	c	9.	d
5.	a	10.	b

Page 50 • People

1.	b	6.	b
2.	d	7.	c
3.	a	8.	d
4.	b	9.	d
5.	d	10.	a

Page 51 • Numbers and Measurement

1.	b	6.	d
2.	a	7.	b
3.	a	8.	a
4.	c	9.	b
5.	d	10.	c